Victoria, Ontario's Babies 1894 - 1895

FORGET ME NOT

Angeline Gallant

Published by Angeline Gallant, 2022.

While every precaution has been taken in the preparation of this book, the publisher assumes no responsibility for errors or omissions, or for damages resulting from the use of the information contained herein.

VICTORIA, ONTARIO'S BABIES 1894 - 1895

First edition. November 5, 2022.

Written by Angeline Gallant.

Also by Angeline Gallant

Calling Her Heart
Whisper of the Heart
No Turning Back
Forsake Me Not
Hear My Cry
Calling Her Heart Boxed Set Volumes 1-4

FORGET ME NOT
Victoria, Ontario's Babies 1894 - 1895

Keeper Of Secrets
A Lady's Secret

Midnight's Awakening
Heart of the Storm
Walking Through The Storm
Midnight's Awakening boxed set volumes 1-3

Secrets of the Underworld
Deklan's Dragons
Secrets of the Underworld Volumes 1 & 2

Tell My Story Collection
Tell My Story: England 1852

The Grave Whisperer
Wedding Bells in Kingston, Ontario, Canada 1923
St. Paul's Anglican Churchyard Kingston, Ontario, Canada A-B
St. Paul's Anglican Churchyard, Kingston, Ontario, Canada C - D
St. Paul's Anglican Churchyard, Kingston, Ontario, Canada G - H
St. Paul's Anglican Churchyard, Kingston, Ontario, Canada J - N
St. Paul's Anglican Churchyard, Kingston, Ontario, Canada O - R
St. Paul's Anglican Churchyard, Kingston, Ontario, Canada S - T
St. Paul's Anglican Churchyard, Kingston, Ontario T - Z
Small Graveyards & Burial Grounds: Kingston, Ontario, Canada
Cataraqui United Church Cemetery 1
Cataraqui United Church Cemetery 2
Cataraqui United Church Cemetary 3
Cataraqui United Church Cemetery 4

The Wolf Whisperer Series
The Cry of the Wolf
Captured Heart
Journey of the Heart

Fate's Legacy
Wolf Whisperer volumes 1 & 2
Endless White
The Wolf Whisperer Volumes 1-4

Standalone
Winds of Change vol 1-3

Watch for more at https://www.goodreads.com/author/show/ 19703964.Angeline_Gallant.

Table of Contents

This book is dedicated to my great-grandmother, Vera (Finnemore) Davidson. May you never be forgotten.

LUCY BETHIA BEATRICE WOODLEY[1]

Lucy was born in Woodville, Victoria, Ontario on February 2, 1895.

~ HENRY FRANCIS WOODLEY[2] ~

Henry was born in Darlington, Ontario on September 3, 1867.

He was three years old when British Columbia joined the confederation in 1871.

Henry was 15 years old when the mining boom in northern Ontario began in 1883.

He was 21 years old when he married Salina on September 19, 1888 in Scugog, Ontario.

Henry was still 21 years old when his sister, Ida May, passed away in 1899.

He was 22 years old when his son, Roy Thompson, was born in 1890.

Henry was 25 years old when his son, Earl Francis, was born in 1893.

He was 27 years old when his daughter, Lucy, was born in 1895. Henry was working as a farmer at that time.

~ SELINA (THOMPSON) WOODLEY[3] ~

Selina was born on Scugog Island on January 13, 1867.

She was 15 years old when the mining boom in northern Ontario began in 1883.

Selina was 20 years old when her sister, Elizabeth Ida, passed away in 1887.

She was 21 years old when she married Henry in Scugog, Ontario on September 19, 1888.

Selina was 22 years old when the Woman's Suffrage movement began in 1890.

She was 23 years old when her son, Roy Thompson, was born in 1890.

Selina was 25 years old when her brother, Aaron, passed away in 1892.

She was 26 years old when her son, Earl Francis, was born on June 5, 1893. Her father passed away on August 25th.

Selina was 28 years old when her daughter, Lucy, was born in 1895.

GEORGE ASHTON WEEKS[4]

George was born on April 22, 1894 in Victoria, Ontario.

~ Charles Edgar Weeks[5] ~

Charles was born in Uxbridge, Ontario on March 3, 1863.

He was two years old when his sister, Ella, passed away in 1865.

Charles was three years old when Ontario was founded on July 1, 1867.

He was 18 years old when his sister, Wilhelmina, passed away in 1881.

Charles was 19 years old when the mining boom in northern Ontario began in 1883.

He was 28 years old when he married Clara in Cannington, Ontario on September 1, 1891.

Charles was 30 years old when his son, Clarence Gladstone, passed away in 1893.

He was 31 years old when his son, George was born in 1934. He was working as a barrister at that time. Charles was Methodist.

~ Clara Anna May Edwards[6] ~

Clara was born in Cannington, Ontario on July 10, 1869.

She was a year old when British Columbia joined the confederation in 1871.

Clara was 13 years old when the mining boom in northern Ontario began in 1883.

She was 22 years old when she married Charles in Cannington, Ontario on September 1, 1891.

Clara was 23 years old when her son, Clarence Gladstone, was born in 1893.

She was 25 years old when her son, George, was born in 1895. Clara was Methodist, but had been Presbyterian previously.

WILLIAM GEORGE McLEOD[7]

Illiam was born on April 29, 1895.

~ NEIL BROWN McLEOD[8] ~

Neil was born in Mariposa, Ontario on July 1, 1848. He was Scottish.

He was 19 years old when Ontario was founded on July 1, 1867.

Neil was 23 years old when British Columbia joined the confederation in 1871.

He was 32 years old when his brother, William, passed away in 1880.

Neil was 35 years old when the mining boom in northern Ontario began in 1883.

He was 43 years old when his daughter, Wilhelmina Georgina, was born in 1891.

Neil was 45 years old when his brother, George, passed away in 1893.

He was 47 years old when his son, William George, was born in 1895. Neil was Presbyterian and a farmer.

~ SARAH MARGARET (STODDART) McLEOD[9] ~

Sarah was born in Brampton, Ontario on October 14, 1858. She was Scottish.

She was eight years old when Ontario was founded on July 1, 1867.

Sarah was 18 years old when her sister, Emma, passed away in 1877.

She was 27 years old when she married Neil on July 21, 1886 in Woodville, Ontario.

Sarah was 31 years old when her father passed away in 1890.

She was 32 years old when her daughter, Wilhelmina Georgina, was born in 1891.

Sarah was 36 years old when her son, William George, was born in 1895.

She was Presbyterian.

GEORGE ANGUS EGO[10]

George was born on May 28, 1895.

~ JOHN PARKER EGO[11] ~

John was born in 1863. He was Scottish.

He was three years old when Ontario was founded on July 1, 1867.

John was 13 years old when his brother, William, passed away in 1877.

He was 26 years old when he married Margaret in Sutton, Ontario on December 26, 1889.

John was 29 years old when his daughter, Lucy Eliza, was born in 1892.

He was 31 years old when his son, George, was born in 1895. John was Presbyterian and worked as a spearist. (Specialist?)

~ MARGARET C. (RIDDELL) EGO "MAGGIE[12] ~

Maggie was born in 1869.

She was a year old when British Columbia joined the confederation in 1871.

Maggie was 20 years old when she married John Parker in Sutton, Ontario on December 26, 1889.

She was 23 years old when her daughter, Lucy Eliza, was born in 1892.

Maggie was 26 years old when her son, George, was born in 1895.

ADA MARIE STABACK[13]

Ada was born in March 1894.

~ ADAM ELLIOT STABACK[14] ~

Adam was born on December 23, 1855.

He was 11 years old when Ontario was founded on July 1, 1867.

Adam was 15 years old when British Columbia joined the confederation in 1871.

He was 25 years old when he married Allison in Victoria, Ontario on January 25, 1881.

Adam was 26 years old when his son, Robert Thomas Paul, was born in 1882 and was 27 years old when he passed away a year later in 1883.

He was 28 years old when his son, James Elliot, was born in 1884.

Adam was 29 years old when his son, Frederick, was born in 1885.

He was 32 years old when his son, Charles Thomas, was born in 1888.

Adam was 34 years old when his son, Robin Maxwell, was born in 1890.

He was 36 years old when his daughter, Pearl, was born in 1892.

Adam was 38 years old when his daughter, Ada Marie, was born in 1894. He was Presbyterian and worked as a postmaster. He'd previously been Anglican.

~ ALLISON DALGLEISH[15] ~

Allison was born in 1857. She was Scottish.

She was 10 years old when Ontario was founded on July 1, 1867.

Allison was 14 years old when British Columbia joined the confederation in 1871.

She was 24 years old when she married Adam Elliot in Victoria, Ontario, on January 25, 1881.

Allison was 37 years old when her daughter Ada Marie was born. She was Presbyterian.

CHARLES HOWARD GOARD[16]

Charles was born on September 15, 1895.

~ RICHARD FRANKLIN GOARD[17]

Richard was born in England in April 1854.

He was 25 years old when he married Sarah Jane in Lindsay, Ontario, on January 21, 1880.

Richard was 26 years old when his son, Thomas Franklin, was born in 1880.

He was 27 years old when his son, Frederick Samuel, was born in 1882.

Richard was 28 years old when the mining boom in northern Ontario took place in 1883. His daughter, Mary Mabel, was born on March 3rd.

He was 30 years old when his daughter, Emma Maria Elizabeth, was born in 1884.

Richard was 32 years old when his daughter, Sadie Alice, was born in 1886.

He was 33 years old when his daughter, Jennie Eva, was born in 1888.

Richard was 36 years old when his son, Arthur Richardson, was born in 1891.

He was 41 years old and a farmer when his son, Charles Howard, was born in 1895.

~ SARAH JANE (RICHARDSON) GOARD[18]

Sarah was born in 1853.

She was 14 years old when Ontario was founded on July 1, 1867.

Sarah was 18 years old when British Columbia joined the confederation in 1871.

She was Baptist.

Sarah was 27 years old when she married Richard Franklin in Lindsay, Ontario on January 21, 1880. Her son, Thomas Franklin, was born in November.

She was 30 years old when her daughter, Mary Mabel, was born in 1883.

Sarah was 31 years old when her daughter, Emma Maria Elizabeth, was born in 1884.

She was 33 years old when her daughter, Sadie Alice, was born in 1886.

Sarah was 35 years old when her daughter, Jennie Eva, was born in 1888.

She was 38 years old when her son, Arthur Richardson, was born in 1891.

Sarah was 42 years old when her son, Charles Howard was born in 1895. By that time she was Presbyterian.

ALICE ELEANOR WESTLAKE[19]

Alice was born on November 9, 1895

~ THOMAS WESTLAKE[20] ~

Thomas was born on September 3, 1861.

He was five years old when Ontario was founded on July 1, 1867.

Thomas was nine years old when British Columbia joined the confederation in 1871.

He was 21 years old when the mining boom in northern Ontario began in 1883.

Thomas was 27 years old when he married Hannah in Huntsville, Ontario, on March 12, 1889.

He was 29 years old when his daughter, Lily Joyce, was born in 1890.

Thomas was 34 years old when his daughter, Alice Eleanor, was born in 1895. He was a farmer.

~ HANNAH (HAWKINS) WESTLAKE[21] ~

Hannah was born in 1862.

She was five years old when Ontario was founded on July 1, 1867.

Hannah was nine years old when British Columbia joined the confederation in 1871.

She was 27 years old when she married Thomas.

Hannah was 29 years old when her daughter, Lily Joyce, was born and 34 years old when Alice Eleanor was born.

HAROLD VINCENT WALDON[22]

Harold was born on October 4, 1895.

~ THOMAS WALDON[23] ~

Thomas was born in May 1866.

He was a year old when Ontario was founded on July 1, 1867.

Thomas was three years old when British Columbia joined the confederation in 1871.

He was 21 years old when his mother passed away in 1888.

Thomas was 28 years old when he married Elizabeth Ellen Neill in Hamilton, Ontario on December 25, 1894.

He was 29 years old when Harold Vincent was born in 1895. Thomas was working as a veterinary surgeon at that time.

~ ELIZABETH ELLEN (NEILL) WALDON[24] ~

Elizabeth was born on September 26, 1868. She was Irish.

She was two years old when British Columbia joined the confederation in 1871.

Elizabeth was 26 years old when she married Thomas in Hamilton, Ontario on December 25, 1894.

She was 27 years old when her son, Harold Vincent, was born in 1895. Elizabeth was Methodist.

JAMES CLIFFORD SARJENT[25]

James was born on March 9, 1895.

~ WILLIAM HENRY SARGENT[26] ~

William was born in England on August 2, 1864.

He was 27 years old when he married Annie Maria on January 13, 1892 in Omenu, Victoria, Ontario.

William was 28 years old when his daughter, Vera Isabella Gwendolyn, was born in 1893.

He was 30 years old when his son, James Clifford, was born in 1895. William was working as a C. P. R. foreman.

~ ANNIE MARIE (BELL) SARGENT[27] ~

Annie was born in Lindsay, Ontario in July 1873.

She was eight years old when the mining boom in northern Ontario began in 1883.

Annie was 16 years old when the Woman's Suffrage movement began in 1890.

She was 20 years old when she married William Henry in Victoria, Ontario on January 13, 1892.

Annie was 22 years old when her daughter, Vera Isabella Gwendolyn was born in 1893.

She was 23 years old when her son, James Clifford, was born in 1895. Annie was a spiritualist.

ETHEL REASLY JENNINGS[28]

Ethel was born on August 14, 1895.

~ THOMAS EDWARD JENNINGS[29] ~

Thomas was working as a hotel keeper when his daughter, Ethel, was born in 1895.

~ MARGARET (WHITLOW) JENNINGS[30] ~

She was Ethel's mother.

BRUCE NEILL THORTON MINNS[31]

Bruce was born on November 11, 1894.

~ DAVID MINNS[32] ~

David was born in October 1857.

He was 13 years old when British Columbia joined the confederation in 1871.

David was 28 years old when he married Margaret in Meaford, Ontario on December 30, 1885. He was Anglican.

He was 29 years old when his son, Randolph Harper Joyce, was born in 1886.

David was 34 years old when his twins, Bessie May and Samuel, were born on May 27, 1892. Samuel passed away the same day.

He was 37 years old and working as a harness maker when his son, Bruce, was born in 1894.

~ MARGARET ELLEN (CLARK) MINNS[33] ~

Margaret was born in 1861. She was Irish.

She was 10 years old when British Columbia joined the confederation in 1871.

Margaret was 20 years old in 1881 and living in Euphrasia, Ontario. She was Presbyterian and a school mistress.

She was 22 years old when the mining boom in northern Ontario began in 1883.

Margaret was 25 years old when she married David in Meaford, Ontario on December 30, 1885.

She was 26 years old when her son, Randolph Harper Joyce, was born in 1886.

Margaret was 32 years old when her twins, Bessie May and Samuel, were born in 1892. Samuel passed away the same day.

She was 34 years old when her son, Bruce, was born in 1894.

BELREDRAH McNABB[34]

Belredrah was born on April 15, 1895.

~ ROBERT A. McNABB[35] ~

Robert was born in Manitoba in September 1870.

He was not yet a year old when British Columbia joined the confederation in 1871.

Robert was 12 years old when the mining boom in northern Ontario took place in 1883.

He was 24 years old and a tailor when his daughter, Belredrah, was born in 1895.

~ BELREDRAH (CAIN) McNABB[36] ~

Belredrah was born in Ontario in November 1871.

She was 11 years old when the mining boom in northern Ontario began in 1883.

Belredrah was 23 years old when her daughter, Belredrah, was born in 1895. She was Presbyterian.

MARY GERTRUDE SCARLETT[37]

Mary was born on March 28, 1895.

~ EDWARD S. SCARLETT[38] ~

Edward was born in Ontario in 1862. He was Irish.

He was five years old when Ontario was founded on July 1, 1867.

Edward was nine years old when British Columbia joined the confederation in 1871.

He was 21 years old when the mining boom in northern Ontario began in 1883.

Edward was 33 years old when his daughter, Mary Gertrude, was born in 1895.

~ JENNETTE MAY (ENGLISH) SCARLETT[39] ~

Jennette was born in 1867. She was Irish.

She was 16 years old when her brother, Sydney, passed away in 1883.

Jennette was 23 years old when her father passed away in 1890.

She was 27 years old when her brother, Henry Wellington, passed away in 1894.

Jennette was 28 years old when her daughter, Mary Gertrude, was born in 1895.

CHARLES DUNCAN KETT[40]

Charles was born on March 13, 1895.

~ WILLIAM HENRY KETT[41] ~

William was born on April 16, 1855.

He was 11 years old when Ontario was founded on July 1, 1867.

William was 24 years old when his daughter, Minnie, was born in 1879.

He was still 24 years old when his sister, Julia Rebecca, passed away in 1880. William was 25 years old when his son, William John, was born a month later on April 29th.

William was 27 years old when his daughter, Mary Eliza, was born in 1882.

He was 29 years old when his daughter, Florence Christina, was born in 1884.

William was 31 years old when his sister, Mary Ann, passed away in 1887. That same year, his daughter, Ann Elizabeth, was born on March 3rd. She passed away the same day.

He was 34 years old when his daughter, Gertrude Livinia, was born in 1889.

William was 36 years old when his son, James Angus, was born in 1892.

He was 39 years old and a farmer when his son, Charles Duncan, was born in 1895.

~ ISABELLA A. (CHISHOLM) KETT[42] ~

Isabella was born in Ontario on May 8, 1863. She was Scottish.

She was three years old when Ontario was founded on July 1, 1867.

Isabella was seven years old when her brother, John Alexander, passed away in 1871.

She was 16 years old when her son, William John, was born in 1880.

Isabella was 19 years old when her daughter, Mary Eliza, was born in 1882.

She was 21 years old when her daughter, Florence Christina, was born in 1884.

Isabella was 23 years old when her daughter, Ann Elizabeth, was born on March 3, 1887. Ann passed away the same day.

She was 26 years old when her daughter, Gertrude Livinia, was born in 1889.

Isabella was 28 years old when her son, James Angus, was born in 1892.

She was 35 years old when her son, Charles Duncan, was born in 1895. Isabella was Presbyterian.

JOHN CARLESS McINTOSH[43]

John was born on May 15, 1895.

~ JOHN McINTOSH[44] ~

John was born in Canada West in 1864. He was Scottish.

He was two years old when Ontario was founded on July 1, 1867.

John was six years old when British Columbia joined the confederation in 1871.

He was eight years old when his mother passed away in 1873.

John was 18 years old when the mining boom in northern Ontario began in 1883.

He was 21 years old when his sister, Margaret, passed away in 1885.

John was 30 years old when his son, John Carless, was born in 1895. He was Presbyterian and a farmer at that time.

~ HARRIETT ELISABETH (KEHOE) McINTOSH[45] ~

Harriett was born in Belleville, Ontario on December 8, 1868. She was Irish.

She was two years old when British Columbia joined the confederation in 1871.

Harriett was 14 years old when the mining boom in northern Ontario began in 1883.

She was 26 years old when her son, John Carless, was born in 1895. Harriett had been Catholic but by this time was Methodist.

GEORGE PERCY GARDNER[46]

George was born on April 1, 1895.

~ WILLIAM GEORGE GARDNER[47] ~

William was born in 1864.

He was two years old when Ontario was founded on July 1, 1867.

William was 22 years old when he married Sarah in Orillia, Ontario, on April 4, 1887.

He was 23 years old when his daughter, Mary Christina Eleanor, was born in 1888.

William was 25 years old when the Women's Suffrage movement began in 1890.

He was 27 years old when his son, John Mark, was born in 1892.

William was 30 years old and a farmer when his son, George Percy, was born in 1895.

~ SARAH (McDONALD) GARDNER[48] ~

Sarah was born in 1867. She was Scottish.

She was 16 years old when her mother passed away in 1883.

Sarah was 19 years old when she married William in Orillia, Ontario on April 4, 1887.

She was 20 years old when her daughter, Mary Christina Eleanor, was born in 1888.

Sarah was 23 years old when her daughter, Florence Sydney, was born in 1890.

She was 24 years old when her son, John Mark, was born in 1892.

Sarah was 27 years old when her son, George Percy, was born in 1895.

MARY MARGARET CAMPBELL[49]

Mary was born on September 7, 1895.

~ JOHN DOUGLAS CAMPBELL[50] ~

John was born in Canada West in June 1864. He was Scottish.

He was two years old when Ontario was founded on July 1, 1867.

John was six years old when British Columbia joined the confederation in 1871.

He was 18 years old when the mining boom in northern Ontario began in 1883.

John was 23 years old when he married Annie on May 31, 1888.

He was 25 years old when his son, William George, was born in 1890. William passed away a year later.

John was 28 years old when his son, James, was born in 1893.

He was 31 years old and a Presbyterian farmer when his daughter, Mary Margaret, was born in 1895.

~ ANNIE WEIR (CAMICK) CAMPBELL[51] ~

Annie was born in New Brunswick, Canada on July 5, 1873. She was Irish.

She was nine years old when her brother, William, passed away in 1882.

Annie was 11 years old when the Canadian Pacific Railway was completed in 1885. Her sister, Maud, passed away on May 16th.

She was 17 years old when she married John on May 31, 1888.

Annie was 19 years old when her son, William George, was born in 1890. He passed away in 1891.

She was 21 years old when her son, James, was born in 1893.

Annie was 24 years old when her daughter, Mary Margaret, was born in 1895.

GRACE BETRICE McLEISH[52]

Grace was born on September 9, 1895.

~ DAVID McLEISH[53] ~

David was born in 1866. He was Scottish.

He was three years old when his brother, Daniel, passed away in 1869. David was a year old.

David was 10 years old when his mother passed away in 1876.

He was 20 years old when his brother, James George, passed away in 1886.

David was 26 years old when he married Mary Alberta in Orillia, Ontario on August 15, 1892.

He was 28 years old when his brother, Donald Daniel, passed away in 1894.

David was 29 years old and a Presbyterian farmer when his daughter, Grace Betrice, was born in 1895.

~ MARY ALBERTA (YOUNG) McLEISH[54] ~

Mary was born in 1874.

She was five years old when her sister, Mabel, passed away in 1880.

Mary was six years old when her brother, William Elmer, passed away in 1881.

She was 18 years old when she married David in Orillia, Ontario on August 15, 1892.

Mary was 21 years old when her daughter, Grace Betrice, was born in 1895.

JAMES LANCELOT BRADEN[55]

James was born on September 12, 1895.

~ THOMAS GEORGE BRADEN[56] ~

Thomas was born in 1864.

He was three years old when Ontario was founded on July 1, 1867.

Thomas was 25 years old when he married Minnie in Orillia, Ontario on July 1, 1889.

He was 26 years old when the Women's Suffrage movement began in 1890. His daughter, Hannah Maye, was born on May 25th.

Thomas was 27 years old when his daughter, Mag, was born in 1891.

He was 30 years old when his son, Noble John, was born in 1893.

Thomas was 31 years old and a farmer when his son, James Lancelot, was born in 1895. He was Methodist.

~ MINNIE (SMITH) BRADEN[57] ~

Minnie was born in 1870.

She was 13 years old when the mining boom in northern Ontario began in 1883.

Minnie was 19 years old when she married Thomas in Orillia, Ontario on July 1, 1889.

She was 20 years old when the Womans' Suffrage Movement began in 1890. Her daughter, Hannah Maye, was born on May 25th.

Minnie was 21 years old when her daughter, Mag, was born in 1891.

She was 24 years old when her son, Noble John, was born in 1893.

Minne was 25 years old when her son, John Lancelot, was born in 1895.

GORDON HENRY FOSTER[58]

Gordon was born on October 29, 1895.

~ THOMAS JAMES FOSTER[59] ~

Thomas was born in 1862. He was Irish.

He was five years old when Ontario was founded on July 1, 1867.

Thomas was nine years old when British Columbia joined the confederation in 1871.

He was 21 years old when he married Eliza in Orillia, Ontario on December 6, 1883.

Thomas was 22 years old when his daughter, Annie, was born in 1884.

He was 25 years old when his son, Thomas Robert, was born in 1887.

Thomas was 28 years old when his son, William, was born in 1890.

He was 29 years old when his daughter, May, was born in 1891.

Thomas was 31 years old when his son, John, was born in 1893.

He was 33 years old and a farmer when his son, Gordon Henry, was born in 1895.

~ ELIZA JANE (CHRYSLER) FOSTER[60] ~

Eliza was Gordon Henry's mother. She was German and Anglican.

DAVID GARDNER LITTLE[61]

David was born on December 8, 1895.

~ JOHN TAYLOR LITTLE[62] ~

John was born in Orillia, Canada West, British Colonial America on April 1, 1861. He was Irish.

He was five years old when Ontario was founded on July 1, 1867.

John was nine years old when British Columbia joined the confederation in 1871.

He was 21 years old when the mining boom in northern Ontario began in 1883.

John was 24 years old when he married Margaret Annie in Simcoe, Ontario on July 13, 1885.

He was 25 years old when his daughter, Minnie Wray, was born in 1886.

John was 27 years old when his daughter, Elizabeth Emma, was born in 1889.

He was 29 years old when his daughter, Annie Gertrude, was born in 1890.

John was 31 years old when his son, James Nelson, was born in 1893.

He was 34 years old and a farmer when his son, David Gardner, was born in 1895.

~ MARGARET ANNIE (GARDINER) LITTLE[63] ~

Margaret was born in 1847. She was Irish.

She was nine years old when Ontario was founded on July 1, 1867.

Margaret was 13 years old when British Columbia joined the confederation in 1871.

She was 28 years old when she married John in Orillia, Ontario on July 13, 1885.

Margaret was 29 years old when her daughter, Minnie Wray, was born in 1886.

She was 31 years old when her daughter, Elizabeth Emma, was born in 1889.

Margaret was 33 years old when her daughter, Annie Gertrude, was born in 1890.

She was 36 years old when her son, James Nelson, was born in 1893.

Margaret was 38 years old when her son, David Gardiner, was born in 1895.

VERA FINNEMORE[64]

Vera was born on February 6, 1895 in Laxton Township, Victoria, Ontario.

~ JOHN FINNEMORE[65] ~

John was born in Otterham, Cornwall, England in 1853.

He was a year old when the Crimean War took place in 1854.

John was 38 years old when his mother passed away in 1891.

He was 42 years old and a farmer when his daughter, Vera, was born in 1895. John was Methodist.

~ FLORA ADDEN (McFADYEN) FINEMORE[66] ~

Flora was born in 1858. She was Scottish

She was eight years old when Ontario was founded on July 1, 1867.

Flora was 12 years old when British Columbia joined the confederation in 1871.

She was 22 years old and working as a servant for Mr. and Mrs. Michael Long in Collingwood, Ontario in 1881. Flora was Presbyterian.

Flora was 23 years old when her father passed away in 1882.

She was 24 years old when the mining boom in northern Ontario took place in 1883.

Flora was 32 years old when she married John in Kirkfield, Ontario on July 23, 1890.

She was 33 years old when her son, Calvin Stanley, was born in 1891.

Flora was 34 years old when her daughter, Mabel, was born in 1893.

She was 36 years old when her daughter, Vera, was born in 1895.

ALICE MAY COOPER[67]

Alice was born on February 16, 1895.

~ GEORGE COOPER[68] ~

George was born in 1833. He was Irish.

He was 22 years old when he married Mary Dixon in Frontenac, Ontario in 1855.

George was 25 years old when his daughter, Margaret Ann, was born in 1858.

He was 26 years old when his son, William James, was born in 1859.

George was 29 years old when his son, Robert, was born in 1862.

He was 30 years old when his wife passed away in 1863.

George was 31 years old when his son, Robert, passed away in 1864. Robert was two years old.

He was 32 years old when he married Ann Catherine Greer in Victoria, Ontario in 1865.

George was 33 years old when his daughter, Esther, was born in 1866. His father also passed away that year.

He was 34 years old when his son, Samuel, was born in 1867.

George was 36 years old when his daughter, Martha, was born in 1869. His son, William James, passed away on November 16th. William was 10 years old.

He was 37 years old when his son, Samuel, passed away in 1870. Samuel was three years old.

George was 38 years old when British Columbia joined the confederation in 1871.

He was 40 years old when his son, William, was born in 1873.

George was 42 years old when his son, Thomas, was born in 1875.

He was 46 years old when his daughter, Elinor Maud, was born in 1879.

George was 49 years old when his daughter, Teeney, was born on September 7, 1882. She passed away two days later on September 9th.

He was 50 years old when the mining boom in northern Ontario began in 1883.

George was 51 years old when his wife passed away in 1884.

He was 58 years old when he married Catherine Henry in Norland, Ontario, on March 31, 1891. Catherine was 38 years old.

George was 59 years old when his son, Edward John, was born in 1892.

He was 62 years old and a farmer when his daughter, Alice May, was born in 1895.

~ CATHERINE (HENRY) COOPER[69] ~

Catherine was born on December 1, 1854. She was German/Irish.

She was 12 years old when Ontario was founded on July 1, 1867.

Catherine was 16 years old when British Columbia joined the confederation in 1871.

She was 18 years old when she married Alexander Lowery in Cannington, Ontario on July 10, 1873. Catherine was 19 years old when her son, George Albert, was born on November 27th.

Catherine was 20 years old when her son, James Alexander, was born in 1875.

She was 22 years old when her daughter, Margaret, was born on May 19, 1877. Margaret passed away the same day.

Catherine was 23 years old when her son, Francis, was born in 1878.

She was 25 years old when her daughter, Margaret Catherine, was born in 1880.

Catherine was 28 years old when her daughter, Francies, was born on February 27, 1883. Francies passed away that same day. Her son, James

Alexander, passed away a few days later on April 2nd. James was eight years old. Two days later, her daughter, Margaret Catherine, passed away on April 4th. Margaret was three years old.

She was 29 years old when her son, James Alexander, was born in 1884.

Catherine was 31 years old when her daughter, Fanny Francis, was born in 1886. She passed away the following year.

She was 34 years old when her son, Hugh Andrew, was born in 1889.

Catherine was 35 years old when her husband passed away in 1890.

She married George Cooper in 1891.

Catherine was 37 years old when her son, Edward John, was born in 1892.

She was 40 years old when her daughter, Alice May, was born in 1895. Catherine was Methodist.

MAGGIE BAILEY[70]

Maggie was born on May 7, 1895.

~ JOHN H. BAILEY[71] ~

John was a farmer when his daughter, Maggie, was born in 1895.

~ CAROLINE O. (KINSLEY) BAILEY[72]

Caroline was Maggie's mother.

EDWARD O'BRIEN[73]

Edward was born on May 25, 1895.

~ EDWARD O'BRIEN[74] ~

Edward was born in Ireland in 1844.

He was French, Catholic, and a farmer when his son, Edward, was born.

Edward was 34 years old when he married Mary Ann in Victoria, Ontario on October 14, 1878. His bride was 17 years old.

~ MARY ANN (McNARNAY) O'BRIEN[75] ~

Mary was born in Carden, Ontario in 1841. She was French.

She was five years old when Ontario was founded on July 1, 1867.

Mary was 17 years old when she married Edward on October 14, 1878.

She was 19 years old when her sons, William and John Joseph, were born in 1881.

Mary was 21 years old when the mining boom in northern Ontario began in 1883.

She was 23 years old when her son, Thomas Frances, was born in 1884.

Mary was 26 years old when her daughter, Teresa, was born in 1888.

She was 34 years old when her son, Edward, was born in 1895. Mary was Catholic.

CATHERINE ISABELLA GROZELLE[76]

Catherine was born on May 26, 1895.

~ ALPHONSE GROZELLE[77] ~

Alphonse was born in Quebec in 1855.

He was 16 years old when British Columbia joined the confederation in 1871.

Alphonse was 21 years old when he married Annie on August 28, 1876.

He was 22 years old when his daughter, Janelle, was born in 1877.

Alphonse was 25 years old when his son, Peter Richard, was born in 1880.

He was 27 years old when his son, Charles Alphonse, was born in 1882.

Alphonse was 28 years old when the mining boom in northern Ontario began in 1883.

He was 29 years old when his son, Gilbert Eric, was born on May 20, 1884. His brothers, Ira Ambrose and Napoleon, passed away on July 11th.

Alphonse was 37 years old when his daughter, Mary Elizabeth, was born in 1892.

He was 38 years old when his father passed away in 1893.

Alphonse was 40 years old and a farmer when his daughter, Catherine Isabella, was born in 1895. He was Catholic.

~ ANNIE (McALPINE) GROZELLE[78] ~

Annie was born on December 15, 1855. She was Scottish.

She was 11 years old when Ontario was founded on July 1, 1867.

Annie was 15 years old when British Columbia joined the confederation in 1871.

She was 18 years old when she married Alphonse on August 28, 1878 in Bexley, Ontario.

Annie was 39 years old when her daughter, Catherine Isabella, was born in 1895. She was Catholic.

WILBERT C. WELLINGTON BOYCE[79]

Wilbert was born on June 3, 1895.

~ SAMUEL JOHN BOYCE[80] ~

Samuel was born on August 29, 1859. He was Irish.

He was seven years old when Ontario was founded on July 1, 1867.

Samuel was 11 years old when British Columbia joined the confederation in 1871.

He was 22 years old when his brother, Joseph, passed away in 1882.

Samuel was 25 years old when his sister, Mary Jane, passed away in 1885.

He was 29 years old when his father passed away in 1889.

Samuel was 29 years old when he married Annie in Kinmount, Ontario on May 23, 1889,

He was 30 years old when his daughter, Lena May, was born in 1890.

Samuel was 32 years old when his mother passed away in 1892.

He was 34 years old when his brother, William, passed away in 1894.

Samuel was 35 years old and a farmer when his son, Wilbert C. Wellington, was born in 1895. He was Presbyterian.

~ ANNIE (GOSTLIN) BOYCE[81] ~

Annie was born on October 30, 1864. She was Dutch/Irish.

She was two years old when Ontario was founded on July 1, 1867.

Annie was six years old when British Columbia joined the confederation in 1871.

She was 18 years old when the mining boom in northern Ontario began in 1883.

Annie was 21 years old when her newborn sibling passed away in 1886.

She was 25 years old when her daughter, Lena, was born in 1890.

Annie was 26 years old when her daughter, Mary Elizabeth, was born in 1891.

She was 30 years old when her son, Wilbert C. Wellington, was born in 1895. Annie was Methodist.

EMILY GERTRUDE NEWMAN[82]

E mily was born on May 5, 1895.

~ JACOB HENRY NEWMAN[83] ~

Jacob was born in Reach, Ontario on September 26, 1861.

He was five years old when Ontario was founded on July 1, 1867.

Jacob was nine years old when British Columbia joined the confederation in 1871.

He was 21 years old when the mining boom in northern Ontario began in 1883.

Jacob was 22 years old when his sister, Ellie Meritta, passed away on November 4, 1883.

He was 28 years old when he married Mary Maria in Lindsay, Ontario, on April 8, 1890.

Jacob was 29 years old when his daughter, Stella Evelyn, was born in 1891.

He was 31 years old when his daughter, Effie, was born in 1893.

Jacob was 32 years old when his one-year-old daughter, Effie, passed away in 1894.

He was 33 years old and a farmer when his daughter, Emily Gertrude, was born in 1895.

~ MARY MARIE (WINTERBURN) NEWMAN[84] ~

Mary was born on February 26, 1870.

She was 12 years old when the mining boom in northern Ontario began in 1883.

Mary was 16 years old when her brother, Frederick Fletcher, passed away in 1886.

She was 20 years old when she married Jacob in Lindsay, Ontario on April 8, 1890.

Mary was 21 years old when her daughter, Stella, was born in 1891.

She was 23 years old when her daughter, Effie, was born in 1893.

Mary was 24 years old when Effie passed away in 1894.

She was 25 years old when her daughter, Emily Gertrude, was born in 1895. Mary was Methodist.

MUNSEL STEWART McLEAN[85]

Munsel was born on June 7, 1895.

~ ARCHIBALD McLEAN[86] ~

Archibald was born in 1862. He was Scottish.

He was four years old when Ontario was founded on July 1, 1867.

Archibald was eight years old when British Columbia joined the confederation in 1871.

He was 20 years old when the mining boom in northern Ontario began in 1883.

Archibald was 30 years old when he married Charlotte Clara on September 5, 1892.

He was 31 years old when his daughter, Margaret Louisa, was born in 1893.

Archibald was 32 years old and a farmer when his son, Munsel, was born on June 7, 1895. Munsel passed away on August 2nd. Archibald was Presbyterian.

~ CHARLOTTE CLARA (WOOLRIDGE) McLEAN[87] ~

Clara was born in England in 1871.

She was 10 years old and a Bible Christian living in Mariposa, Ontario in 1881.

Clara was 22 years old when her daughter, Margaret Louisa, was born in 1893.

She was 24 years old when her son, Munsel, was born on June 7, 1895.

HARRIET ELEY HOSKINS[88]

Harriet was born on October 24, 1895.

~ RICHARD HOSKIN[89] ~

Richard was born in Canada West in 1844.

He was a year old when his brother, William, passed away in 1846.

Richard was eight years old when his sister, Susanna, passed away in 1852.

He was 26 years old when British Columbia joined the confederation in 1871.

Richard was 42 years old when he married Sarah Jane in 1887.

He was 51 years old and a farmer when his daughter, Harriett, was born in 1895. Richard was Methodist.

~ SARAH JANE (WICKS) HOSKIN[90]

Sarah was born in Ontario, Canada in 1867.

She was 20 years old when she married Richard in 1887.

Sarah was 28 years old when her daughter, Harriet, was born in 1895. She was Methodist.

OSWARD HENRY LEE[91]

Osward was born on June 14, 1895.

~ GEORGE LEE[92] ~

George was born in Limehouse, England in 1848.

He was three years old when his mother passed away in 1852.

George was 37 years old when he married Emma Alberta in Queensville, Ontario on June 17, 1885.

He was 38 years old when his daughter, Hannah Maude, was born in 1886.

George was 39 years old when his daughter, Lizzie Janette, was born in 1887.

He was 41 years old when his son, William George, was born in 1890.

George was 43 years old when his daughter, Eliza Alberta, was born in 1891.

He was 46 years old and a farmer when his son, Oswald Henry, was born in 1895.

~ EMMA ALBERTA (LINSTEAD) LEE[93] ~

Emma was born in East Gwillimbury in June 1864.

She was 16 years old when her sister, Geanette, passed away in 1880.

Emma was 21 years old when she married George in Queensville, Ontario in 1885.

She was 31 years old when her son, Oswald Henry, was born in 1895.

ELIZA JANE WESSELS[94]

Eliza was born on June 18, 1895.

~ ISAAC HENRY WICKS[95] ~

Isaac was born in Brighton Township, Ontario on December 1, 1860.

He was 10 years old when British Columbia joined the confederation in 1871.

Isaac was 20 years old when his sister, Ann, passed away in 1881.

He was 22 years old when the mining boom in northern Ontario began in 1883.

Isaac was 34 years old and a farmer when his daughter, Eliza Jane, was born in 1895. He was Methodist.

~ SILVA JANE (WESSALS) WICKS[96] ~

Silva was born in Victoria, Ontario on February 26, 1870. She was Dutch.

She was five years old when her brother, James Allen, passed away in 1876.

Silva was 12 years old when the mining boom in northern Ontario took place in 1883.

She was 20 years old when her sister, Mary, passed away in 1890.

Silva was 25 years old when her daughter, Eliza Jane, was born in 1895. She was Methodist.

[1] https://www.wikitree.com/genealogy/Woodley-Family-Tree-581

[2] https://www.wikitree.com/genealogy/Woodley-Family-Tree-282

[3] https://www.wikitree.com/genealogy/Thompson-Family-Tree-26585

[4] https://www.wikitree.com/genealogy/Weeks-Family-Tree-7531

[5] https://www.wikitree.com/genealogy/Weeks-Family-Tree-7532

[6] https://www.wikitree.com/genealogy/Edwards-Family-Tree-38117

[7] https://www.wikitree.com/genealogy/McLeod-Family-Tree-8268

[8] https://www.wikitree.com/genealogy/McLeod-Family-Tree-8269

[9] https://www.wikitree.com/genealogy/Stoddart-Family-Tree-813

[10] https://www.wikitree.com/genealogy/Ego-Family-Tree-31

[11] https://www.wikitree.com/genealogy/Ego-Family-Tree-30

[12] https://www.wikitree.com/genealogy/Riddell-Family-Tree-2210

[13] https://www.wikitree.com/genealogy/Staback-Family-Tree-3

[14] https://www.wikitree.com/genealogy/Stabak-Family-Tree-1

[15] https://www.wikitree.com/genealogy/Dalgleish-Family-Tree-513

[16] https://www.wikitree.com/genealogy/Goard-Family-Tree-121

[17] https://www.wikitree.com/genealogy/Goard-Family-Tree-120

[18] https://www.wikitree.com/genealogy/Richardson-Family-Tree-34545

[19] https://www.wikitree.com/genealogy/Westlake-Family-Tree-284

[20] https://www.wikitree.com/genealogy/Westlake-Family-Tree-283

[21] https://www.wikitree.com/genealogy/Howskins-Family-Tree-2

[22] https://www.wikitree.com/genealogy/Waldon-Family-Tree-407

[23] https://www.wikitree.com/genealogy/Waldon-Family-Tree-406

[24] https://www.wikitree.com/genealogy/Neill-Family-Tree-2403

[25] https://www.wikitree.com/genealogy/Sargent-Family-Tree-5504

[26] https://www.wikitree.com/genealogy/Sargent-Family-Tree-5503

[27] https://www.wikitree.com/genealogy/Bell-Family-Tree-39018

[28] https://www.wikitree.com/genealogy/Jennings-Family-Tree-13250

[29] https://www.wikitree.com/genealogy/Jennings-Family-Tree-13249

[30] https://www.wikitree.com/genealogy/Whitlow-Family-Tree-829

[31] https://www.wikitree.com/genealogy/Minns-Family-Tree-406

[32] https://www.wikitree.com/genealogy/Minns-Family-Tree-405

[33] https://www.wikitree.com/genealogy/Clark-Family-Tree-77023

[34] https://www.wikitree.com/genealogy/McNabb-Family-Tree-1646

[35] https://www.wikitree.com/genealogy/McNabb-Family-Tree-1645

[36] https://www.wikitree.com/genealogy/Cain-Family-Tree-8446

[37] https://www.wikitree.com/genealogy/Scarlett-Family-Tree-926

[38] https://www.wikitree.com/genealogy/Scarlett-Family-Tree-422

[39] https://www.wikitree.com/genealogy/English-Family-Tree-6393

[40] https://www.wikitree.com/genealogy/Kett-Family-Tree-292

[41] https://www.wikitree.com/genealogy/Kett-Family-Tree-291

[42] https://www.wikitree.com/genealogy/Chisholm-Family-Tree-3361

[43] https://www.wikitree.com/genealogy/McIntosh-Family-Tree-7273

[44] https://www.wikitree.com/genealogy/McIntosh-Family-Tree-7272

[45] https://www.wikitree.com/genealogy/Kehoe-Family-Tree-883

[46] https://www.wikitree.com/genealogy/Gardner-Family-Tree-20969

[47] https://www.wikitree.com/genealogy/Gardner-Family-Tree-20968

[48] https://www.wikitree.com/genealogy/McDonald-Family-Tree-27564

[49] https://www.wikitree.com/genealogy/Campbell-Family-Tree-55059

[50] https://www.wikitree.com/genealogy/Campbell-Family-Tree-55057

[51] https://www.wikitree.com/genealogy/Camick-Family-Tree-17

[52] https://www.wikitree.com/genealogy/McLeish-Family-Tree-412

[53] https://www.wikitree.com/genealogy/McLeish-Family-Tree-411

[54] https://www.wikitree.com/genealogy/Young-Family-Tree-54967

[55] https://www.wikitree.com/genealogy/Braden-Family-Tree-1334

[56] https://www.wikitree.com/genealogy/Braden-Family-Tree-1333

[57] https://www.wikitree.com/genealogy/Smith-Family-Tree-289263

[58] https://www.wikitree.com/genealogy/Foster-Family-Tree-31915

[59] https://www.wikitree.com/genealogy/Foster-Family-Tree-31913

[60] https://www.wikitree.com/genealogy/Chrysler-Family-Tree-271

[61] https://www.wikitree.com/genealogy/Little-Family-Tree-20584

[62] https://www.wikitree.com/genealogy/Little-Family-Tree-20583

[63] https://www.wikitree.com/genealogy/Gardiner-Family-Tree-5551

[64] https://www.wikitree.com/genealogy/Finemore-Family-Tree-11

[65] https://www.wikitree.com/genealogy/Finemore-Family-Tree-13

[66] https://www.wikitree.com/genealogy/McFadyen-Family-Tree-203

[67] https://www.wikitree.com/genealogy/Cooper-Family-Tree-37355

[68] https://www.wikitree.com/genealogy/Cooper-Family-Tree-37353

[69] https://www.wikitree.com/genealogy/Henry-Family-Tree-16768

[70] https://www.wikitree.com/genealogy/Bailey-Family-Tree-36854

[71] https://www.wikitree.com/genealogy/Bailey-Family-Tree-36850

[72] https://www.wikitree.com/genealogy/Kinsley-Family-Tree-427

[73] https://www.wikitree.com/genealogy/O'Brien-Family-Tree-12785

[74] https://www.wikitree.com/genealogy/O'Brien-Family-Tree-12784

[75] https://www.wikitree.com/genealogy/McNarnay-Family-Tree-1

[76] https://www.wikitree.com/genealogy/Grozelle-Family-Tree-67

[77] https://www.wikitree.com/genealogy/Grozelle-Family-Tree-10

[78] https://www.wikitree.com/genealogy/McAlpine-Family-Tree-319

[79] https://www.wikitree.com/genealogy/Boyce-Family-Tree-4322

[80] https://www.wikitree.com/genealogy/Boyce-Family-Tree-4321

[81] https://www.wikitree.com/genealogy/Gostlin-Family-Tree-40

[82] https://www.wikitree.com/genealogy/Newman-Family-Tree-13600

[83] https://www.wikitree.com/genealogy/Newman-Family-Tree-13599

[84] https://www.wikitree.com/genealogy/Winterburn-Family-Tree-387

[85] https://www.wikitree.com/genealogy/McLean-Family-Tree-10819

[86] https://www.wikitree.com/genealogy/McLean-Family-Tree-10806

[87] https://www.wikitree.com/genealogy/Woolridge-Family-Tree-400

[88] https://www.wikitree.com/genealogy/Hoskins-Family-Tree-3480

[89] https://www.wikitree.com/genealogy/Hoskin-Family-Tree-972

[90] https://www.wikitree.com/genealogy/Wicks-Family-Tree-1881

[91] https://www.wikitree.com/genealogy/Lee-Family-Tree-42112

[92] https://www.wikitree.com/genealogy/Lee-Family-Tree-42111

[93] https://www.wikitree.com/genealogy/Linstead-Family-Tree-50

[94] https://www.wikitree.com/genealogy/Wessels-Family-Tree-4371

[95] https://www.wikitree.com/genealogy/Wicks-Family-Tree-1882

[96] https://www.wikitree.com/genealogy/Wessals-Family-Tree-1

Don't miss out!

Visit the website below and you can sign up to receive emails whenever Angeline Gallant publishes a new book. There's no charge and no obligation.

https://books2read.com/r/B-A-QGSI-UWOCC

BOOKS 2 READ

Connecting independent readers to independent writers.

Also by Angeline Gallant

Calling Her Heart
Whisper of the Heart
No Turning Back
Forsake Me Not
Hear My Cry
Calling Her Heart Boxed Set Volumes 1-4

FORGET ME NOT
Victoria, Ontario's Babies 1894 - 1895

Keeper Of Secrets
A Lady's Secret

Midnight's Awakening
Heart of the Storm
Walking Through The Storm
Midnight's Awakening boxed set volumes 1-3

Secrets of the Underworld
Deklan's Dragons
Secrets of the Underworld Volumes 1 & 2

Tell My Story Collection
Tell My Story: England 1852

The Grave Whisperer
Wedding Bells in Kingston, Ontario, Canada 1923
St. Paul's Anglican Churchyard Kingston, Ontario, Canada A-B
St. Paul's Anglican Churchyard, Kingston, Ontario, Canada C - D
St. Paul's Anglican Churchyard, Kingston, Ontario, Canada G - H
St. Paul's Anglican Churchyard, Kingston, Ontario, Canada J - N
St. Paul's Anglican Churchyard, Kingston, Ontario, Canada O - R
St. Paul's Anglican Churchyard, Kingston, Ontario, Canada S - T
St. Paul's Anglican Churchyard, Kingston, Ontario T - Z
Small Graveyards & Burial Grounds: Kingston, Ontario, Canada
Cataraqui United Church Cemetery 1
Cataraqui United Church Cemetery 2
Cataraqui United Church Cemetary 3
Cataraqui United Church Cemetery 4

The Wolf Whisperer Series
The Cry of the Wolf
Captured Heart
Journey of the Heart

Fate's Legacy
Wolf Whisperer volumes 1 & 2
Endless White
The Wolf Whisperer Volumes 1-4

Standalone
Winds of Change vol 1-3

Watch for more at https://www.goodreads.com/author/show/
19703964.Angeline_Gallant.

www.ingramcontent.com/pod-product-compliance
Lightning Source LLC
Chambersburg PA
CBHW061633130726
47996CB00003B/1257